D1174794

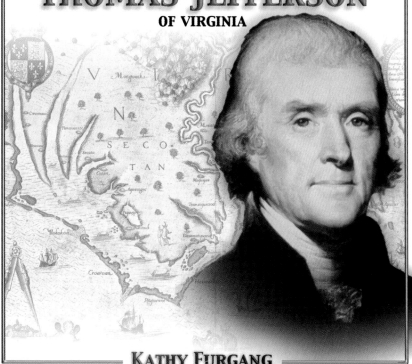

THE DECLARATION OF INDEPENDENCE AND
THOMAS JEFFERSON
OF VIRGINIA

KATHY FURGANG

The Rosen Publishing Group's
PowerKids Press™
New York

For Adam

Published in 2002 by The Rosen Publishing Group, Inc.
29 East 21st Street, New York, NY 10010

First Edition

Book design: Maria E. Melendez

Photo credits: Cover and title page, Portrait of Thomas Jefferson © Bettmann/CORBIS; title page, map of Virginia © SuperStock; title page, the Declaration of Independence document © North Wind Pictures; pp. 4, 15 (Portrait of Thomas Jefferson), 16 (Signers of the Declaration of Independence) © Bettmann/CORBIS; pp. 7 (Still life objects), 12 (Drafting the Declaration of Independence) © SuperStock; pp. 8 (Stamp Act at Boston), 11 (Monticello, Thomas Jefferson's home, Charlottesville VA), 19 (Map showing land claims of the 13 original states, 1783), 20 (Washington in 1810–inset of the old capital) © North Wind Pictures.

Furgang, Kathy.
    The Declaration of Independence and Thomas Jefferson of Virginia / Kathy Furgang. — 1st ed.
       p. cm. — (Framers of the Declaration of Independence)
    Includes index.
    ISBN 0-8239-5589-3
    1. United States. Declaration of Independence—Juvenile literature. 2. Jefferson, Thomas, 1743–1826—Juvenile literature. 3. United States—Politics and government—1775–1783—Juvenile literature.
    [1. United States. Declaration of Independence—Signers. 2. Jefferson, Thomas, 1743–1826. 3. Presidents. 4. United States—Politics and government—1775–1783.] I. Title.
    E221 .F95 2002
    973.3'13—dc21   00-011863
Manufactured in the United States of America

CONTENTS

This is a portrait of Thomas Jefferson in the late 1700s.

A GREAT AMERICAN

Thomas Jefferson was born in a Virginia farmhouse on April 2, 1743. Thomas's father showed him how to farm, hunt, and fish. He also taught Thomas how to read books. Thomas loved to read outside, on a hilltop near his home. Thomas was very well educated. He had **tutors** who taught him to read in French, Greek, and Latin. He learned to play the violin and to dance. He also studied science, literature, and math. When Thomas grew up, he became one of the most famous Americans in history.

YOUNG THOMAS JEFFERSON

When Thomas was 14, his father died. Thomas could not stay at home after his father died. He had to continue his schooling. He spent seven years at the College of William and Mary. When Thomas was 19, he began to study law. Thomas became a lawyer in 1767. One law that troubled Thomas very much was the law that stated that the country of England had control over the American **colonies**.

These are books and school supplies from the 1700s. At that time, people dipped feather quills in ink and wrote with them.

THE FOLLY OF ENGLAND
AND THE RUIN OF AMERICA

The colonists protested one tax, the Stamp Tax, so strongly that King George of England took back the tax less than a year after it was passed.

BEFORE AMERICA WAS A COUNTRY

When Thomas was young, America was made up of colonies that were controlled by England. England was across the Atlantic Ocean, 3,000 miles (4,828 km) away. King George of England, passed laws that the **colonists** thought were unfair. Colonists in America had to pay **taxes** to England. Colonists were not allowed to have any say about the taxes or about laws that were passed. This made many colonists angry. The American colonists began to talk about freeing themselves from England.

REPRESENTING VIRGINIA

Thomas Jefferson was tall and skinny, with red hair and freckles. He was not a strong speaker, but he was a very good writer. Thomas wanted to help the colonies become free. He wrote booklets and newspaper articles about freedom. In 1769, Thomas was elected a member of Virginia's House of Burgesses. The House of Burgesses was part of the government in the colony of Virginia. Being a part of the House of Burgesses meant that Thomas had to **represent** the ideas of the people of Virginia.

In 1772, Thomas got married to a woman named Martha Skelton. Thomas and Martha moved into a house that Thomas had designed when he was only 27 years old. Thomas named the house Monticello. This is Monticello today.

This is (left to right) Benjamin Franklin, John Adams, and Thomas Jefferson, working on the Declaration of Independence.

THE COLONIES WANT FREEDOM

In 1774, representatives from the colonies got together in Philadelphia to discuss the future of the colonies. The **American Revolution** began in 1775. In June of 1776, the men met again in Philadelphia. This time, they picked five men to write a **document** declaring the colonies free from England. These men were John Adams, Roger Sherman, Robert Livingston, Benjamin Franklin, and young Thomas Jefferson. The document was to be called the Declaration of Independence. The Declaration would become famous all around the world.

13

WRITING THE
DECLARATION OF INDEPENDENCE

At first, John Adams was chosen to write the document. John wanted Thomas to write it. John said to Thomas, "you are 10 times better a writer than I am." Thomas worked hard and wrote a beautiful document. The Declaration said that all people are equal. This may not sound surprising to us, but it was a very new idea at that time. Thomas also wrote that the slave trade should be ended. The other representatives did not approve that idea. It would be another 100 years before slaves were freed.

Thomas studied the ideas of great thinkers when he was young. He wanted this new country to put those ideas into practice. For example, he did not think people needed a king to rule them. Thomas believed the people should rule themselves.

(left to right) John Adams, Thomas Jefferson, and Benjamin Franklin offer the Declaration of Independence to Congress.

THE ROAD TO INDEPENDENCE

On July 4, 1776, the members of **Congress** approved the Declaration. We still celebrate every July 4th as Independence Day. The Declaration was copied onto handmade paper called parchment and passed out among the colonies. People read the document out loud at town meetings. Generals read the Declaration to their soldiers to remind them of why they were fighting.

The American Revolution ended in 1781. There was a lot to be done in the new country. Thomas's work was far from over.

NEW LAWS FOR VIRGINIA

Thomas served as the **governor** of the new state of Virginia from 1779 until 1781. As the governor, Thomas helped to make laws for the state. One of these laws allowed more people to own land. Only people who owned land were allowed to vote. The more people who owned land, the fairer the voting would become. It was also Thomas Jefferson who began the idea of free public schools in America. In 1781, Thomas took three years off to be with his family and to work on his farm.

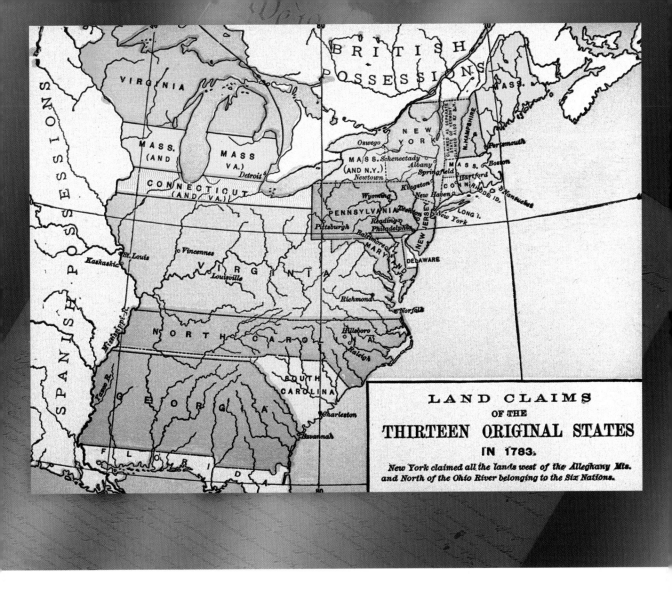

These are the 13 original states in the Union. Many laws that began in Virginia were later used in other states.

These people are gathered to watch Thomas become the president in 1801. The building is the unfinished Capitol building in Washington, D.C.

THE THIRD PRESIDENT OF THE UNITED STATES

After his wife Martha died in 1782, Thomas returned to politics. From 1784 to 1789, Thomas represented the United States in France. In 1796, Thomas ran against his friend John Adams for the presidency. John Adams won the race. At that time, the second place candidate became the vice president, and so Thomas became John Adams' vice president. Four years later, Thomas was elected to be the third president of the United States. He was elected to serve a second term as president in 1804.

A MAN OF GREAT IDEAS

Thomas spent the last years of his life at Monticello with his children and grandchildren. He died on July 4, 1826. This was the same day that his friend John Adams died in Massachusetts. Both men died exactly 50 years after the Declaration of Independence was signed. Thomas was 83 years old, and John Adams was 92. Today Thomas Jefferson is remembered as one of the most important people in our country's history.

GLOSSARY

American Revolution (ah-MER-ih-kuhn REH-vuh-loo-shun) The war that American colonists fought from 1775 to 1783 to win independence from England.

colonies (KAH-luh-neez) An area in a new country where a large group of people move who are still ruled by the leaders and laws of their old country.

colonists (KAH-luh-nists) The people who live in a colony.

Congress (KON-gres) The part of the United States government that makes laws and is made up of the House of Representatives and the Senate.

document (DOHK-yoo-ment) An official piece of writing.

governor (GUH-vuh-nur) An official that is put in charge of a colony by a king or queen.

represent (reh-prih-ZENT) To stand for.

slaves (SLAYV) A person who is "owned" by another person and is forced to work for him or her.

taxes (TAKS-ez) Money that people give the government to help pay for public services.

tutors (TOO-terz) Someone who teaches one student or a small group of students.

INDEX

WEB SITES

To learn more about Thomas Jefferson and the Declaration of Independence, check out these Web sites:

http://www.historyplace.com/unitedstates/revolution/decindep.htm

http://www.monticello.org/